Our Holidays

Celebrate Thanksgiving

Elizabeth Lawrence

Cavendish
Square

New York

Published in 2016 by Cavendish Square Publishing, LLC
243 5th Avenue, Suite 136, New York, NY 10016

Copyright © 2016 by Cavendish Square Publishing, LLC

First Edition

CPSIA Compliance Information: Batch #WS15CSQ

All websites were available and accurate when this book was sent to press.

Library of Congress Cataloging-in-Publication Data

Lawrence, Elizabeth.
Celebrate Thanksgiving / by Elizabeth Lawrence.
p. cm. — (Our holidays)
Includes index.
ISBN 978-1-50260-413-2 (hardcover) ISBN 978-1-50260-412-5 (paperback)
ISBN 978-1-50260-414-9 (ebook)
1. Thanksgiving Day — Juvenile literature. 2. United States — Social life and customs — Juvenile literature. I. Lawrence, Elizabeth, 1988-. II. Title.
GT4975.L366 2016
394.2649—d23

Editorial Director: David McNamara
Editor: Kristen Susienka
Copy Editor: Cynthia Roby
Art Director: Jeffrey Talbot
Designer: Joseph Macri
Senior Production Manager: Jennifer Ryder-Talbot
Production Editor: Renni Johnson

The photographs in this book are used by permission and through the courtesy of: Ray Kachatorian/Getty Images, cover; © Cavendish Square, 5; Frederic Lewis/Archive Photos/Getty Images, 7; Lambert/Hulton Fine Art Collection/Getty Images, 9; fstop123/E+/Getty Images, 11; YinYang/E+/Getty Images, 13; Brian Chase/Shutterstock.com, 15; MSPhotographic/Shutterstock.com, 17; Cultura/Jakob Helbig/Riser/Getty Images, 19; Monkey Business Images/Shutterstock.com, 21.

Printed in the United States of America

Contents

Today is Thanksgiving.

Thanksgiving is the fourth
Thursday of November.

4

NOVEMBER

Sunday	Monday	Tuesday	Wednesday	Thursday	Friday	Saturday
1	2	3	4	5	6	7
8	9	10	11	12	13	14
15	16	17	18	19	20	21
22	23	24	25	26	27	28
29	30					

The first Thanksgiving was a special **meal**.

It was shared by **Pilgrims** and **Native Americans**.

The Pilgrims left Europe to live in America.

Native Americans taught them how to grow food.

9

Today we celebrate Thanksgiving with family and friends.

10

Abby and Anna help cook food for Thanksgiving.

13

We eat turkey on Thanksgiving.

14

15

Pumpkin pie is fun to eat, too.

17

Hannah helps set the table.

18

Family and friends eat
Thanksgiving meals together.

Happy Thanksgiving!

New Words

meals (MEELz) Food eaten at breakfast, lunch, or dinner.

Native Americans (NAY-tiv a-MER-ih-kanz) The first people to live in America.

Pilgrims (PILL-grimz) A group of people who came to America in the 1600s to start new lives.

Index

23

About the Author

Elizabeth Lawrence lives in Albany, New York. She likes to write books, celebrate holidays with family and friends, and cook.

About BOOKWORMS

Bookworms help independent readers gain reading confidence through high-frequency words, simple sentences, and strong picture/text support. Each book explores a concept that helps children relate what they read to the world in which they live.